The People's Power

Copyright ©2024 by Honored Abilities
| One of the People Called Charle
Published 2024 by Honored Abilities
www.honoredabilities.com
Cover Design: Everett Escobar | Honored Abilities
Illustrations :Everett Escobar | Honored Abilities
|Aerias Hurd

The People's Power is not intended to have any resemblance to actual people, events, places, or incidents. Any resemblance is completely coincidental
All rights reserved.

"For my heirs-may they forever live a life of abundance and prosperity."

"We but mirror the world. All the tendencies present in the outer world are to be found in the world of our body. If we could change ourselves, the tendencies in the world would also change. As a man changes his own nature, so does the attitude of the world change towards him. This is the divine mystery supreme. A wonderful thing it is and the source of our happiness. We need not wait to see what others do."

~ Mahatma Gandhi

"Educate and inform the whole mass of the people... They are the only sure reliance for the preservation of our liberty."

- Thomas Jefferson

"A frequent recurrence to fundamental principles, and a firm adherence to justice, virtue, and original law, are indispensably necessary to preserve the blessings of liberty and good government..."
(American Maxim 51q)

"The construction of the law (a construction made by the law) works no injury. The law will make such a construction of an instrument as not to injure a party."
(Maxim of Law 22e)

You were born with *inalienable rights* that can never be taken away from you without YOUR consent.

It's important to know your rights in order to protect them, and stand up for yourself, ensuring you're treated fairly and respectfully.

What are inalienable rights?

Inalienable means something that cannot be taken or given away.. Inalienable rights are fundamental freedoms inherent to every human, not granted by law but born with us.
Every constitution lists a few fundamental rights which are inalienable rights.

What are a few of the people's inalienable rights?

- The right to acquire, possess, & protect one's property

- The right to pursue happiness in a lawful manner

- The right to a clean & healthy environment

- The right to enjoy & defend one's life

- The right to peaceably to assemble, and to petition the Government for a redress of grievances.

Each state has a **bill or declaration of rights** which acknowledge the People's Power. With this power comes responsibility.

All people are by nature ***free and independent*** and have **inalienable rights**. Among these are enjoying and defending life and liberty, acquiring, possessing, and protecting property, and pursuing and obtaining safety, happiness, and privacy.

California Constitution Article I - Declaration of Rights Section 1.

TEXAS BILL OF RIGHTS
ARTICLE 1 SECTION 1

Freedom and Sovereignty of State

Texas is a free and independent State, subject only to the Constitution of the United States, and the maintenance of our free institutions and the perpetuity of the Union depend upon the preservation of the right of local self-government, unimpaired to all the States.

TEXAS BILL OF RIGHTS
Article 1 Section 2
Source of Political Power

"That all political power is vested in and derived from the people; that all government of right originates from the people, is founded upon their will only, and is instituted solely for the good of the whole."

HAWAII BILL OF RIGHTS
Article 1 Section 1
Political Power

"All political power of this State is inherent in the people and the responsibility for the exercise thereof rests with the people. All government is founded on this authority."

VIRGINIA DECLARATION OF RIGHTS
ARTICLE 1 SECTION 2

"That all power is vested in, and consequently derived from, the people, that magistrates are their trustees and servants, and at all times a amenable to them."

The state's Bill of Rights or Declaration of Rights, might use different words, but they all talk about the fundamental truth that power originates from the people, highlighting their inherent responsibility in its governance.

MISSOURI BILL OF RIGHTS
ARTICLE 1 SECTION 2

Promotion of General Welfare--Natural Rights of Persons-Equality Under the Law-Purpose of Government

"That all constitutional government is intended to promote the general welfare of the people; that all persons have a natural right to life, liberty, the pursuit of happiness and the enjoyment of the gains of their own industry; that all persons are created equal and are entitled to equal rights and opportunity under the law; that to give security to these things is the principal office of government, and that when government does not confer this security, it fails in its chief design"

VIRGINIA DECLARATION OF RIGHTS
People the Source of Power

"That all power is vested in, and consequently derived from, the people, that magistrates are their trustees and servants, and at all times amenable to them"

HAWAII BILL OF RIGHTS
Rights of Individuals

"All persons are free by nature and are equal in their inherent and inalienable rights. Among these rights are the enjoyment of **life, liberty and the pursuit of happiness**, and the acquiring and possessing of property. These rights cannot endure unless the people recognize their corresponding obligations and responsibilities-"

The states Bill of Rights or Declaration of Rights, might use different words, but they all talk about the fundamental truth that power originates from the people, highlighting their inherent responsibility in its governance.

These are only the first two sections from four of fifty state constitutions. It's important to read your state's entire Bill, or Declaration of Rights to get a grasp of most of your rights, powers, and responsibilities.

MAXIMS RELATED TO GOVERNMENT

All political power is inherent in the people by decree of God, thus none can exist except it be derived from them. *(American Maxim)*
(Maxim of Law 51o)

The main object of government is the protection and preservation of personal rights, private property, and public liberties, and upholding the law of God. *(American Maxim)*
(Maxim of Law 51p)

As usurpation is the exercise of power, which another has a right to; so tyranny is the exercise of power beyond right, which no body can have a right to. *(Locke, Treat. 2, 18, 199.)*
(Maxim of Law 51r)

All Maxims of Law used within this book are derived from: Weisman, Charles A. Maxims of Law: An English Version (1990).

The people have been led to believe that they are under the authority of the government. The truth is that the government/ all public servants and trustees are under the authority of the people.
Public servants and trustees have pledged to serve the people faithfully; acknowledging that the true power lies in the hands of the people.

THE VIRGINIA DECLARATION OF RIGHTS
Article 1 Section 1

Equality and Rights of Men

"That all men are by nature equally free and independent and have certain inherent rights, of which, when they enter into a state of society, they cannot, by any compact, deprive or divest their posterity; namely, the enjoyment of life and liberty, with the means property, and pursuing and obtaining happiness and safety. "

Reading other state constitutions is valuable because it helps people better comprehend their own power and responsibilities.

The people decided to share some of their power for their benefit.

"That government is, or ought to be, instituted for the common benefit, protection, and security of the people, nation, or community; of all the various modes and forms of government, that is best which is capable of producing the greatest degree of happiness and safety, and is most effectually secured against the danger of maladministration; and, whenever any government shall be found inadequate or contrary to these purposes, a majority of the community hath an indubitable, inalienable, and indefeasible right to reform, alter, or abolish it, in such manner as shall be judged most conducive to the public weal."

Virginia Bill of Rights Article 1 Section 3

The people from different states came together to make the United States Constitution.

"We the People of the United States, in Order to form a more perfect Union, establish Justice, insure domestic Tranquility, provide for the common defense, promote the general Welfare, and secure the Blessings of Liberty to ourselves and our Posterity, do ordain and establish this Constitution for the United States of America-"

(Preamble of the United States Constitution)

The Constitution established **three branches of government** in each state and the United States: the **legislative, executive, and judicial branches.**

1. Legislative Branch:

This is like the top boss of the government. It's responsible for making laws. The legislative branch is made up of Congress, which includes the House of Representatives and the Senate. They are supposed to listen to the people's ideas, debate them, and then vote on whether to make them into laws.

2. Executive Branch:

This branch is led by the President, who is like the boss of the country. The executive branch enforces the laws made by Congress. The President also has other important duties, such as making sure the country is safe and representing the United States to other countries.

3. Judicial Branch:

This branch is like the referee. It's made up of the courts, including the Supreme Court. The judicial branch is responsible for settling disputes by acting in the people's best interest, ensuring that the people's secured rights remain protected.

"This Constitution, and the Laws of the United States which shall be made in Pursuance thereof; and all Treaties made, or which shall be made, under the Authority of the United States, shall be the supreme Law of the Land; and the Judges in every State shall be bound thereby, anything in the Constitution or Laws of any State to the Contrary notwithstanding."

The United States Constitution: Article VI Paragraph 2: *Supremacy Clause*

There are several constitutions that acknowledge that the Constitutions are a special trust created for the benefit of the people.

"All political power is inherent in the people, and all free governments are founded on their authority, and instituted **for their benefit**; and they have at all times an undeniable and indefeasible right to alter their form of government in such manner as they may think expedient."
**CONNECTICUT CONSTITUTION:
ARTICLE 1: SECTION 2**

"All political power is inherent in the people. Government is **instituted for their equal protection and benefit**, and they have the right to alter, reform, or abolish the same, whenever they may deem it necessary; and no special privileges or immunities shall ever be granted, that may not be altered, revoked, or repealed by the General Assembly."
**OHIO CONSTITUTION:
ARTICLE 1 SECTION 2**

"All power is inherent in the people, and all free governments are founded on their authority and instituted **for their peace, safety and happiness**. For the advancement of these ends they have at all times an inalienable and indefeasible right to alter, reform or abolish their government in such manner as they may think proper."

**PENNSYLVANIA CONSTITUTION
ARTICLE 1 SECTION 2**

"We declare that all men, when they form a social compact are equal in right: that all power is inherent in the people, and all free governments are founded on their authority, and instituted for their **peace, safety, and happiness**; and they have at all times a right to alter, reform, or abolish the government in such manner as they may think proper"

**OREGON CONSTITUTION
ARTICLE 1 SECTION 1**

Think of a **Trust** as a treasure chest. Inside of this treasure chest are all the important rules and promises that help keep things fair and safe for the people.

As a **trust** protector, your job is to make sure that the treasure chest stays safe and that the rules inside are followed by everyone.

The government has an important job.

Powers of the People over Internal Affairs, Constitution and Form of Government

That the people of this state have the **inherent, sole** and **exclusive right** to regulate the internal government and police thereof, and to alter and abolish their constitution and form of government whenever they may deem it necessary to their safety and happiness, provided such change be not repugnant to the Constitution of the United States.

**MISSOURI CONSTITUTION:
ARTICLE 1 SECTION 3**

Object of Government

The people of this state have the **inherent right** of regulating their internal government. Government is instituted for the protection, security, and benefit of the people; and at all times they have the right to alter or reform the same whenever the public good may require it.

**GEORGIA CONSTITION:
ARTICLE 1 SECTION 2 PARAGRAPH II**

The government has an important job (continued).

Government for the People; They May Change It

That government is, or ought to be, instituted for the common benefit, protection, and security of the people, nation, or community, and not for the particular **emolument** or advantage of any single person, family, or set of persons, who are a part only of that community; and that the community hath an **indubitable, unalienable,** and **indefeasible right**, to reform or alter government, in such manner as shall be, by that community, judged most conducive to the public weal.

VERMONT CONSTITUTION: ARTICLE 7

Political Power; Purpose of Government

All political power is inherent in the people, and governments derive their just powers from the consent of the governed, and are established to protect and maintain individual rights

ARIZONA CONSTITUTION: ARTICLE 2 SECTION 1

All public servants and trustees express their consent to be governed by taking an oath to uphold both the United States Constitution and the Constitution of the State before entering public service.

The derivative power cannot be greater that the the original from which it is derived.
Maxim of Law 11b

Maxim 691.
To know a thing, and to be bound to know it, are regarded in law as equivalent.

"Government being instituted for the common benefit, protection, and security, of the whole community, and not for the private interest or emolument of any one man, family, or class of men; therefore, whenever the ends of government are perverted, and public liberty manifestly endangered, and all other means of redress are ineffectual, the people may, and of right ought to reform the old, or establish a new government. The doctrine of nonresistance against **arbitrary power**, and **oppression**, is **absurd,** slavish, and destructive of the good and happiness of mankind".

New Hampshire Constitution: Section 1 Article 10

Imagine you have a toy car, and your friend wants to borrow it. You let your friend borrow the toy car, but you tell them they can't make any changes to it or use it in ways that you wouldn't want. That's because the toy car belongs to you, and you're the one who decides how it's used. In the same way, the people let the government borrow their power and the constitutions tell them what they can and can't do with that power. They have to follow the rules and not go beyond them, just like with your toy car.

The government is supposed to promote the general welfare of the people.

Promotion of General Welfare--Natural Rights of Persons-Equality Under the Law--Purpose of Government

"That all constitutional government is intended to promote the general welfare of the people; that all persons have a natural right to **life, liberty, the pursuit of happiness** and the enjoyment of the gains of their own industry; that all persons are created equal and are entitled to equal rights and opportunity under the law; that to give security to these things is the principal office of government, and that when government does not confer this security, it fails in its chief design."

**MISSOURI CONSTITUTION:
ARTICLE 1 SECTION 3**

Several Constitutions Acknowledge Inherent Rights, and the Government's Duty to Protect Them

Object of Government

The people of this state have the **inherent right** of regulating their internal government. Government is instituted for the protection, security, and benefit of the people; and at all times they have the right to alter or reform the same whenever the public good may require it.

**GEORGIA CONSTITUTION:
ARTICLE 1 SECTION 2 PARAGRAPH II**

The People have a Right to Due Process and Remedy.

DUE PROCESS AND EQUAL PROTECTION

No person shall be deprived of life, liberty or property without due process of law nor be denied the equal protection of the laws.

ILLINOIS BILL OF RIGHTS: ARTICLE 4

Access to Courts

The courts shall be open to every person for redress of any injury, and **justice shall be administered without sale, denial or delay**

FLORIDA BILL OF RIGHTS: ARTICLE 1 SECTION 21

**Article 1 Section 29
Texas Bill of Rights**

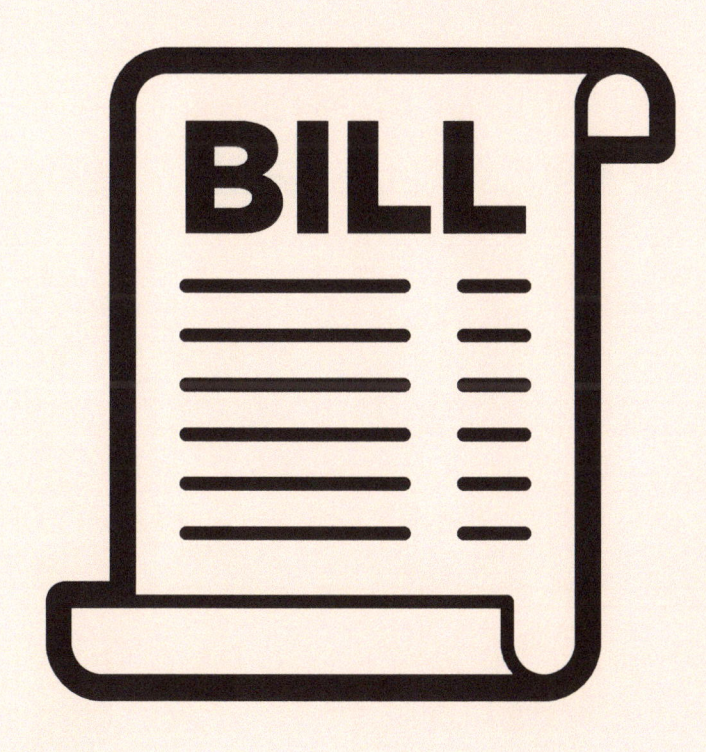

"To guard against transgressions of the high powers herein delegated, we declare that every thing in this **"Bill of Rights"** is excepted out of the general powers of government, and shall forever remain inviolate, and all laws contrary thereto, or to the following provisions, shall be void."

LET'S BREAK DOWN THE PREVIOUS PAGE.
Delegated" is another way to say "assigned" or "entrusted."

"Excepted" is another way of saying not included

"inviolate" is another way of "saying" safe or "untouched"

"Contrary" is another way of saying "opposite" or "different from."

"Void" is another way of saying "empty" or "without anything." In this case, it also means "invalid" or "not legally binding."

Which means that every thing in the **"Bill of Rights"** or **"Declaration of rights"** is not included in the entrusted powers of the government and that the people's rights shall forever be safe and untouched and that anything opposite of the bill or declaration of rights is invalid.

Another way to put it is; everything listed in the **"Bill of Rights"** or **"Declaration of Rights"** isn't controlled by the government's assigned powers. The People's rights will always be protected and can't be changed. Anything that goes against what's in these documents is considered invalid.

Constitutions don't grant rights; rather, they secure and protect certain rights. All of the people's rights aren't mentioned but they're still protected .

"That this enumeration of certain rights shall not impair or deny others retained by the people; and, to guard against any encroachments on the rights herein retained, we declare that everything in this **Declaration of Rights** is excepted out of the general powers of government, and shall forever remain inviolate."

**Alabama Declaration of Rights:
Section 1 Section 36**

"Wherever law ends, tyranny begins, if the law be **transgressed** to another's harm; and whosoever in authority exceeds the power given him by the law, and makes use of the force he has under his command to compass that upon the subject which the law allows not, ceases in that to be a magistrate, and acting without authority may be opposed, as any other man who by force invades the right of another."

Section 202 of "Two Treatises of Government"
By: John Locke

When public servants /trustees don't follow the law, it can lead to damages and injury.
If someone in public service breaks the law and violates their oath they're not really in public service anymore. They're just acting like a bully without authority. It's up to the people to stand up for what's right.

The United States Constitution, and the State Constitutions, to which all **public servants** and trustees swear an oath, serves as a safeguard for the rights of the people. No **public servant** or **trustee** has the authority granted by the people to violate the rights secured by these constitutions.

All **public servants** and **trustees**, upon taking their oaths of office, pledge to support, protect, preserve, and defend the United States Constitution and the State Constitutions. These constitutions serve as the guardians of the rights and liberties of the people, and it is the duty of **public servants** to uphold and honor them.

...These rights cannot endure unless the people recognize their corresponding obligations and responsibilities

**Article 1
Section 2 Hawaii Constitution**

If **public servants** and trustees fail to fulfill their sworn duties outlined in the constitutions, it is the responsibility of the people to tell them what's wrong and give them a chance to fix it.

This ensures that **public servants** remain **accountable** to the people they serve and preserves our Constitutional Republic.

When **public servants or trustees** refuse to listen to the concerns of the people (their bosses), the people have the right to assemble to redress **grievances**. When lots of people join in, it can make a big difference because there's strength in numbers.

The people have at all times the *inalienable right* to alter, reform or abolish their government in such manner as they may think expedient.

Right to Assemble and Petition:
The people have the right peaceably to assemble for the common good, and to apply to those invested with the powers of government for redress of grievances, by petition or remonstrance.
**Colorado Constitution:
Article 2 Section 24**

In any disagreement or uncertainty about a law, it's crucial to consult the Constitution and Maxims of Law. The Constitution is the supreme law of the land, outlining the delegated powers and limits of government. By referring to it, we can determine the true meaning of laws and how they should be followed.

A Maxim is: an established principle, or a principle of law universally admitted, as being a correct statement of the law, or as agreeable to natural reason. "A court can only declare what the law is, and whether consistent with the law of God, and the fundamental or constitutional law of society."
Maxim of Law **64ff**

The people are entitled to due process under common law. When people encounter legal challenges due to conflicts between **statutes** and constitutional rights, the court is breaking the law by regarding one of the people as something other than one the people they swore an oath to benefit. If the people don't assert their status as 'the people,' the court can bypass their rights by presuming them to be something else. Such as a government created person subject to statues and codes.

Just as **Luke 11:52 (KJV)** states; lawyers "have taken away the key of knowledge…" By changing definitions and withholding the common law from the public, the people have become vulnerable to the pitfalls of void statutes and codes, unaware of their secured rights under the Constitutions and the common law.

41

Knowing your rights and responsibilities is necessary in safeguarding the trust instituted for the people's benefit.

Empowered with knowledge, the people can actively participate in shaping a just and equitable community where their rights are respected and upheld.

42

It's important to recognize that a significant portion of the population remains unaware of their rights. Therefore, it falls upon us to engage in conversations and share knowledge about the Constitutions and our rights with others; by spreading awareness and having discussions, we can empower individuals to assert their rights and contribute to the establishment of a better government that truly serves the best interests of the people, governed by the people themselves.

Studying fundamental law, informs the people of their rights and responsibilities

Here are some actionable steps the people can take:

- Read your state and other state's Constitutions s as well as the United States Constitution
- Learn the power of an **Affidavit**
- Read A selection of **Maxims** of Law By Charles Weisman
- Be willing to communicate with public servants/Trustees and challenge them publicly on where they get the authority to do the things they do.
- Let all public **servants/Trustees** know that they can no longer go against the people.
- Attend Town hall meetings
- Get your town's charter and read it- can be found online.
- Exercise your right to alter, reform or abolish the government and remove **public servants/trustees** who don't want to work for the people's benefit from office.
- Keep judges on watch, attend court cases and note any violations of the people's rights.

Studying fundamental law, informs the people of their rights and responsibilities (continued)

Here are some actionable steps the people can take:
- ***visit http://restoremyrepublic.com/***
- ***visit https://wethepeoplenotices.org/***
- Look up your states legislative rules to determine which legislative procedure manual is used and read it.

"The advancement and diffusion of knowledge is the only guardian of true liberty"
James Madison

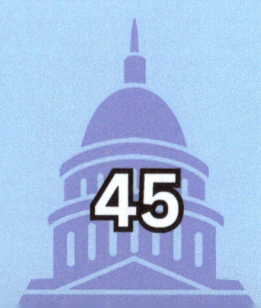

Power Words

- **Affidavit -** *written declaration upon an oath.*
- **Emolument -** *the profit arising from office or employment.*
- **Servant -** *a person who performs duties for others.*
- **Trustee -** *person who is responsible for the property of another*
- **Assemble -** *meet or come together.*
- **Petition -** *make a request to.*
- **Inalienable Rights -** *rights possessed by virtue of human nature.*
- **Accountable -** *answerable, "literally" liable to be called to account.*
- **Grievance -** *an official statement of a complaint over something believed to be wrong or unfair.*
- **Maxim -** *is an established principle or principle of law universally admitted as being a correct statement of the law, or as agreeable to the natural reason.*

Power Words (Continued)

- **inherent Rights -** *rights that cannot be taken or given away.*
- **Trangressed -** *an act that goes against the law.*
- **Bill of Rights -** *a list of secured rights.*
- **Declaration of Rights -** *a list of secured rights.*
- **Arbitrary Power -** *absolute power with no external control.*
- **Oppression -** *cruel or unjust use of power or authority.*
- **Absurd -** *unreasonable, illogical, inappropriate.*

Works Cited (Beyond the Listed Constitution Articles)

Weisman, Charles. A Selection of Maxims of Law: An English Version. Weisman Publications, 1990.

Locke, John. Two Treatises of Government. Awnsham Churchill, 1689.

The Holy Bible: King James Version. Zondervan, 2017. (Original work published 1611)

Notes

About the Author

Charle is a child of God who enjoys reading.